STEP-BY-STEP
Measurement, Fractions, and Graphs

LINWORTH LEARNING

From the Minds of Teachers

Linworth Publishing, Inc.
Worthington, Ohio

Cataloging-in-Publication Data

Editor: Claire Morris

Design and Production: Good Neighbor Press, Inc.

Published by Linworth Publishing, Inc.
480 East Wilson Bridge Road, Suite L
Worthington, Ohio 43085

ISBN: 1-58683-142-9

5 4 3

Table of Contents

# Introduction

The goal of this book is the development of skills in measurement, fractions, and graphing for the Pre-K–2 student. Competency is achieved through fun, step-by-step, practice exercises presented in a variety of formats to accommodate individual learning styles. The consistent use of pictures to illustrate mathematical concepts enhances children's ability to grasp mathematical ideas. Activity sheets have clear and simple instructions and examples, and are written at low readability levels to promote success and understanding. Assessment activities follow the format of standardized tests and require students to eliminate incorrect options, choose the correct answer, and fill in the appropriate circle. The material in *Step-by-Step Measurement, Fractions, and Graphs* correlates with the relevant national curriculum standards for the Pre-K–2 student set by the National Council of Teachers of Math. An answer key is provided at the back of the book.

Measurement

Directions: Write how many inches long each worm is.

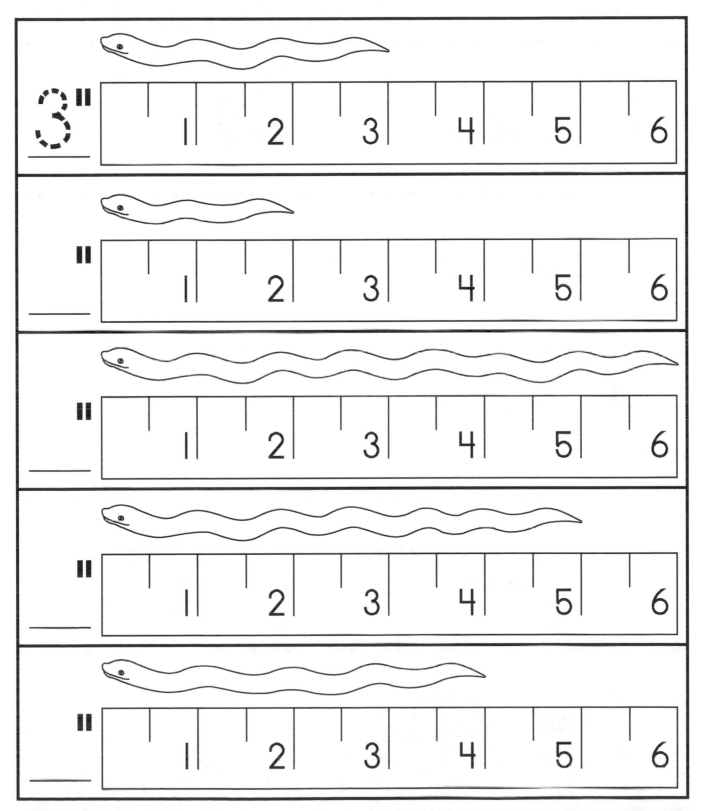

Name_____ Date_____

Measurement

Directions: Use a ruler to measure. Write how many inches long each picture is.

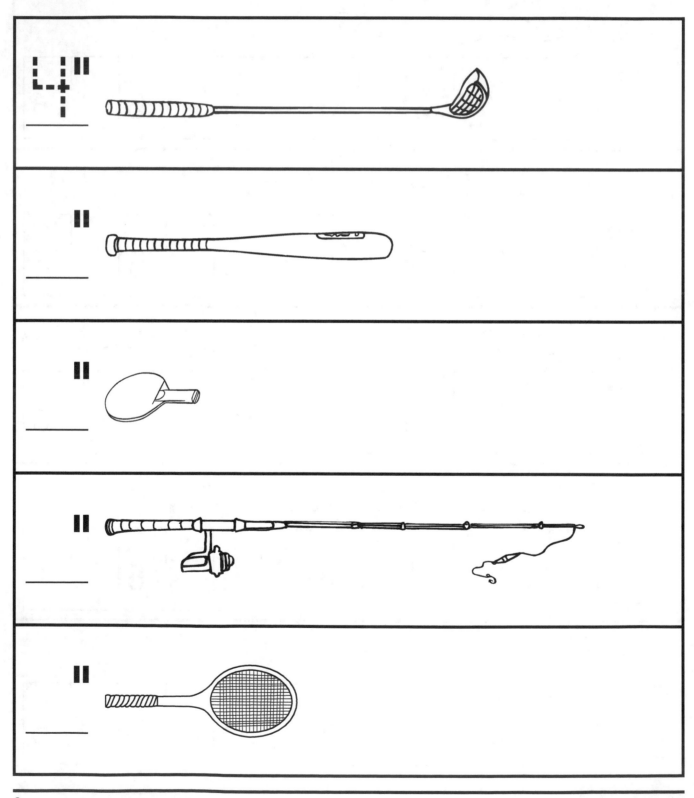

Measurement

Directions: Write the number of degrees each thermometer shows.

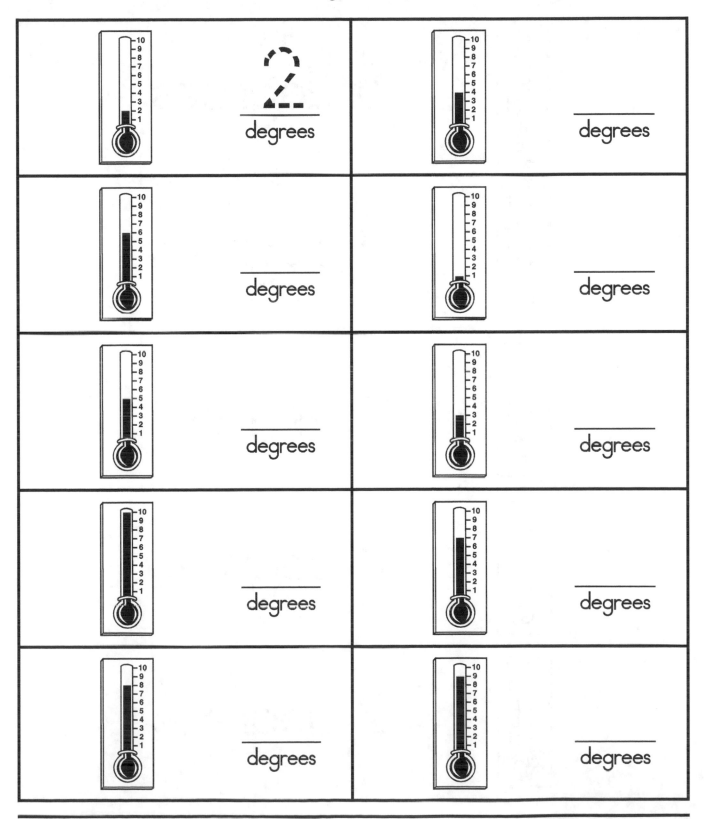

2
degrees

_____ degrees

_____ degrees

_____ degrees

_____ degrees

_____ degrees

_____ degrees

_____ degrees

_____ degrees

_____ degrees

Measurement

Directions: Color each thermometer to match the number of degrees.

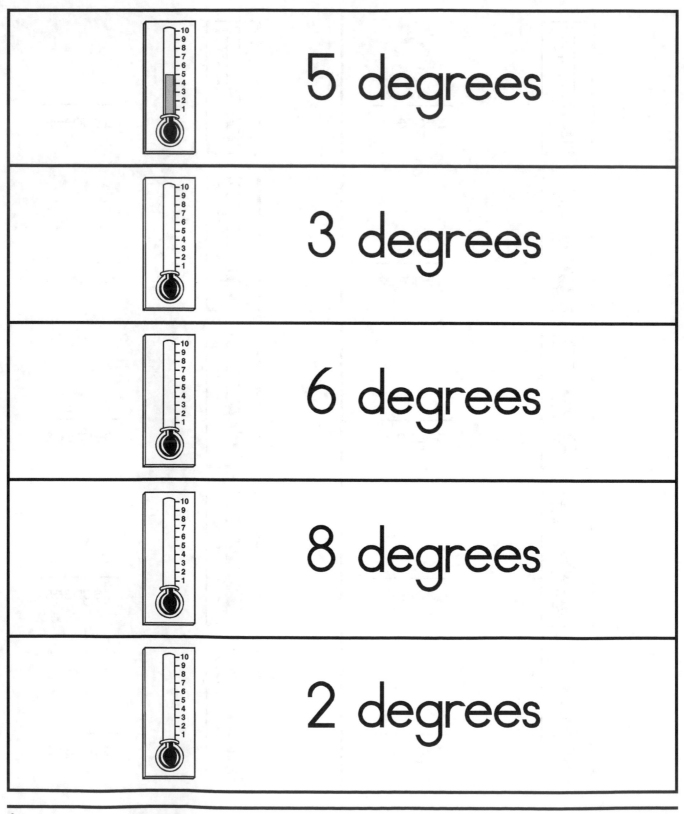

5 degrees

3 degrees

6 degrees

8 degrees

2 degrees

Name_____ Date_____

Measurement

Directions: Circle the thermometer that matches the number of degrees.

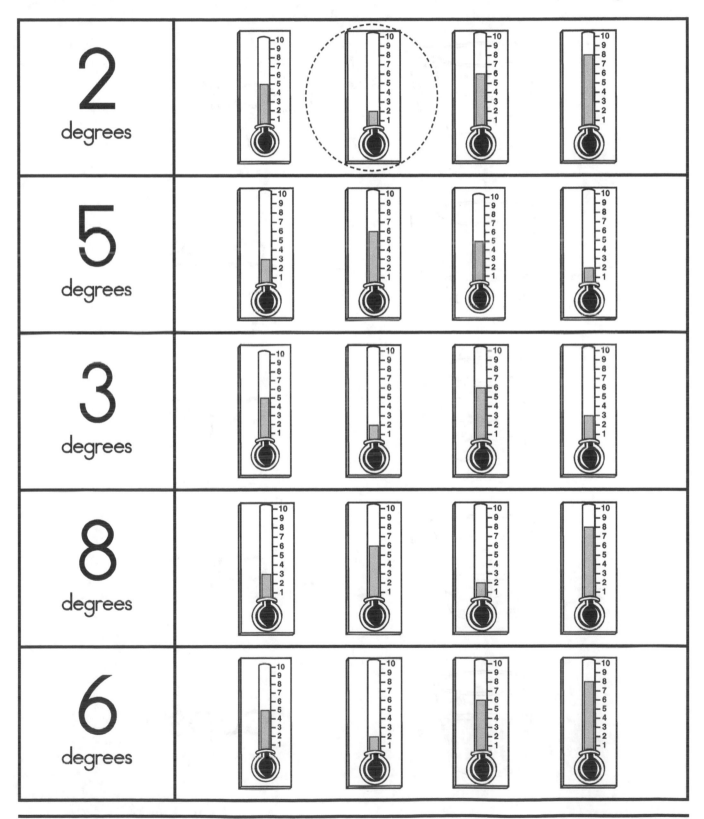

Measurement

Directions: Write the number of cups that are in each measuring cup.

_____ cup

_____ cups

_____ cups

_____ cups

_____ cups

Measurement

Directions: Color each measuring cup to match the number of cups.

3 cups

4 cups

2 cups

5 cups

1 cup

Measurement

Directions: Circle the measuring cup that matches the number of cups.

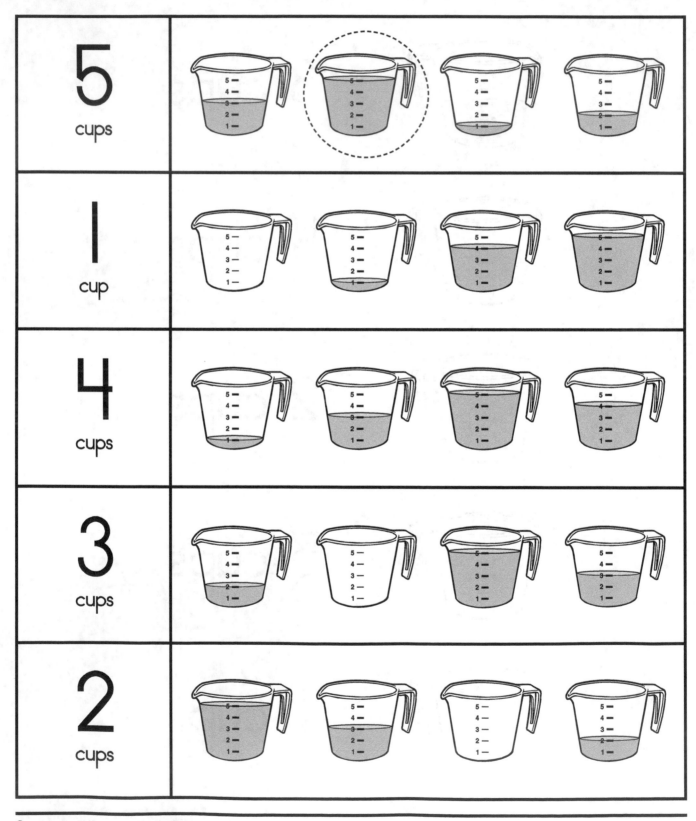

Name________________________ Date________________________

Measurement

Directions: Write the number of pounds that are shown on each scale.

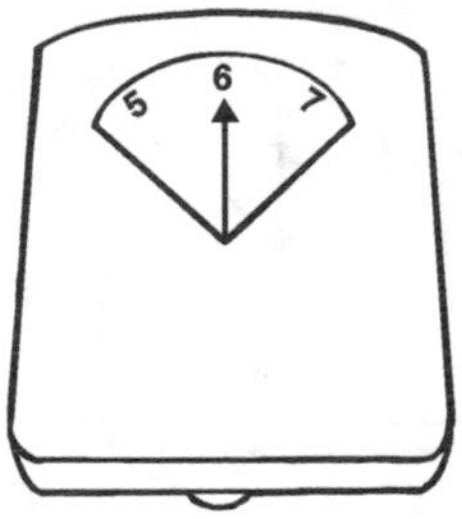

6 pounds

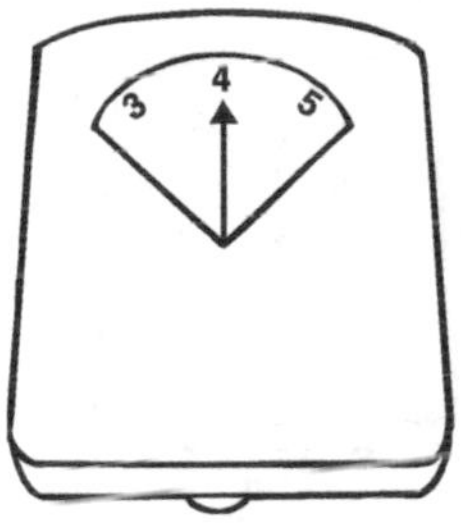

___ pounds

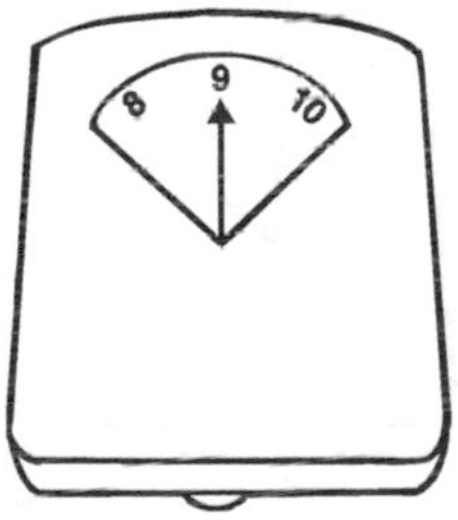

___ pounds

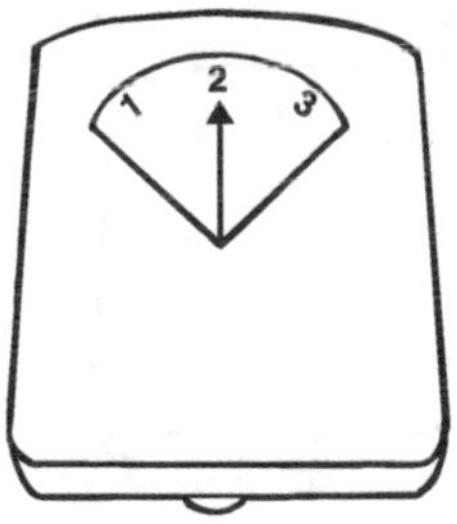

___ pounds

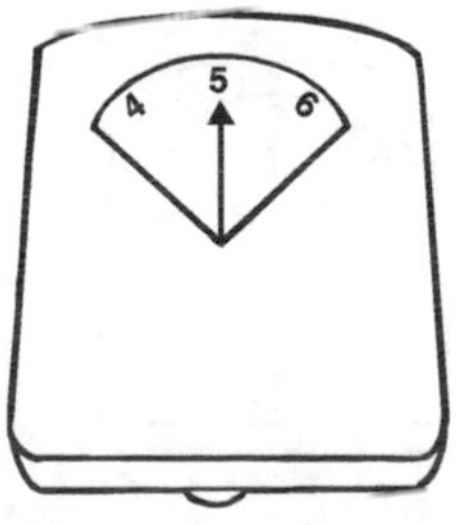

___ pounds

Measurement

Directions: Circle the scale that matches the number of pounds.

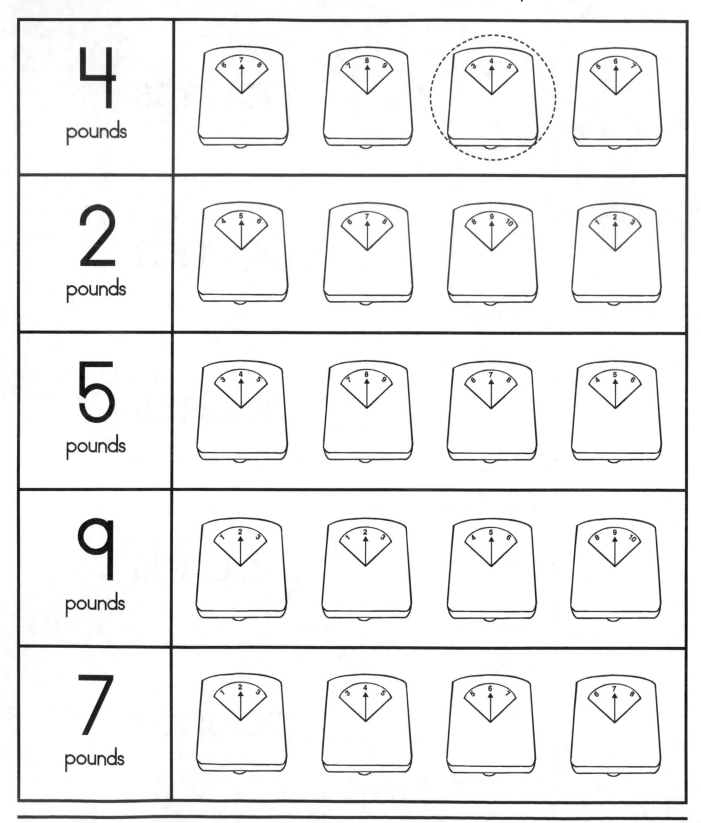

Measurement

Directions: Write the number of pounds that are shown on each scale.

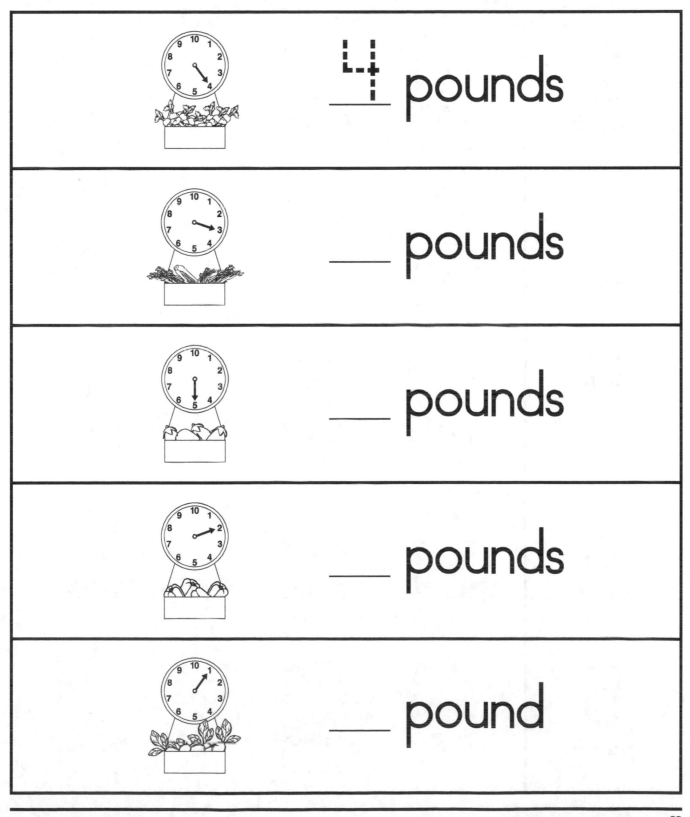

4 pounds

___ pounds

___ pounds

___ pounds

___ pound

Name_____ Date_____

Measurement

Directions: Circle the scale that matches the number of pounds.

2 pounds				
1 pound				
4 pounds				
3 pounds				
5 pounds				

Measurement

Directions: Circle the picture that weighs more.

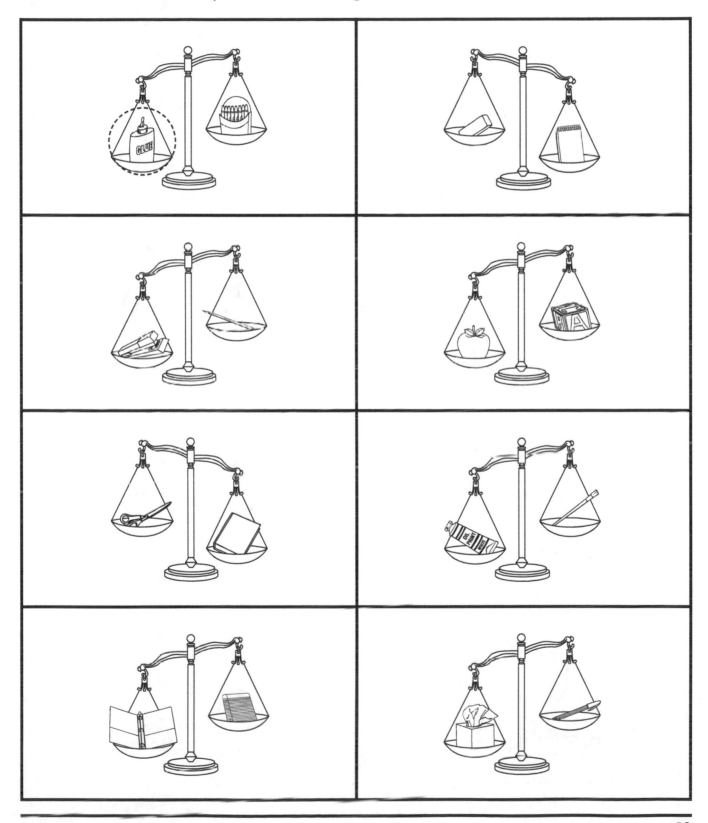

Measurement

Directions: Circle the picture that weighs less.

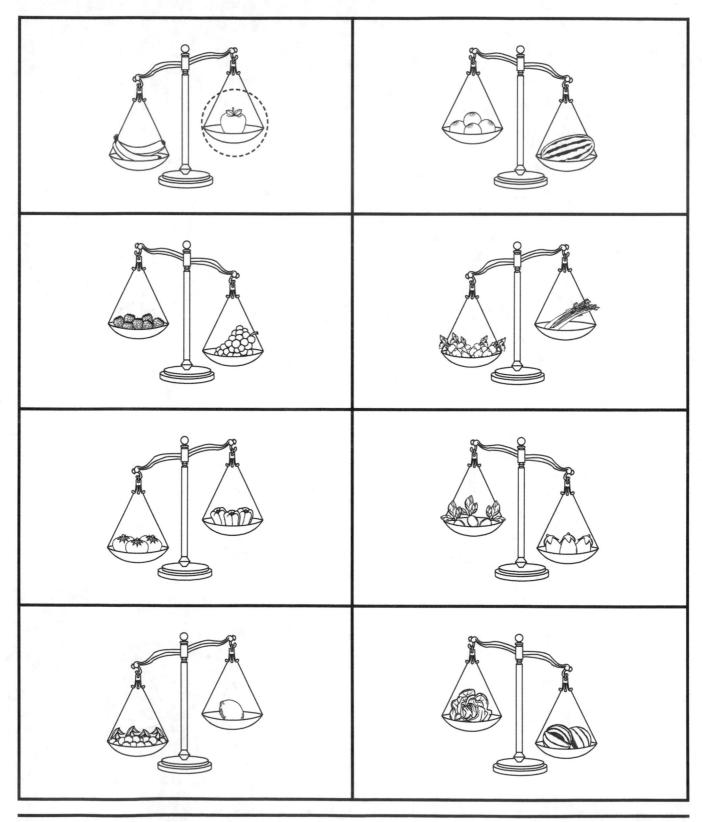

Name________________________________ Date________________________

Measurement

Directions: Circle the picture that matches the measurement.

5 degrees	
2 pounds	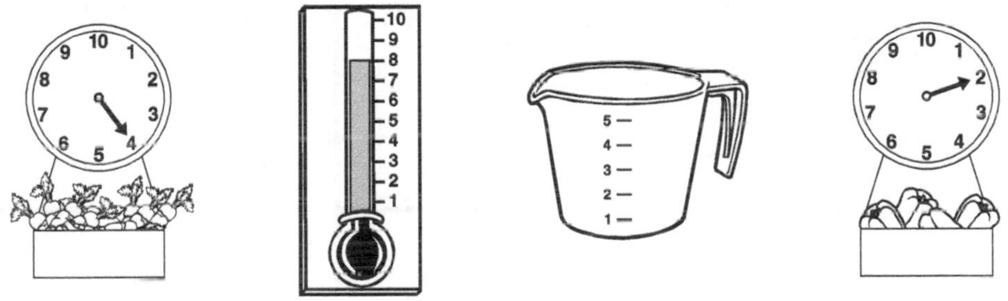
3 cups	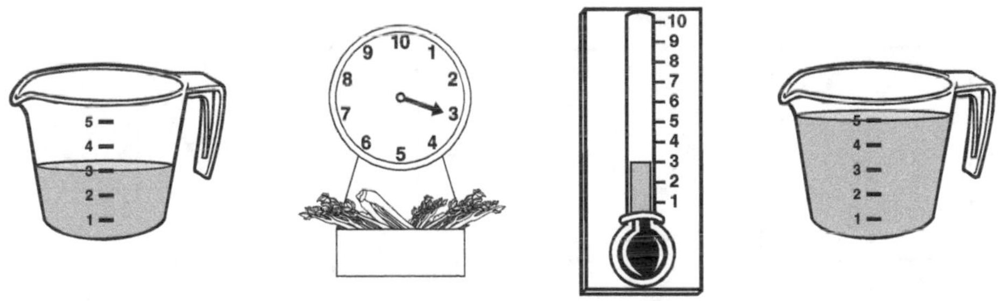
6 degrees	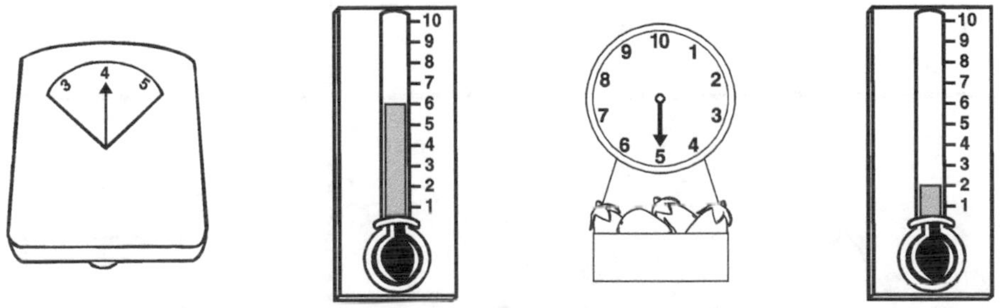
4 cups	

Equal Parts

Directions: Circle the shape that has equal parts.

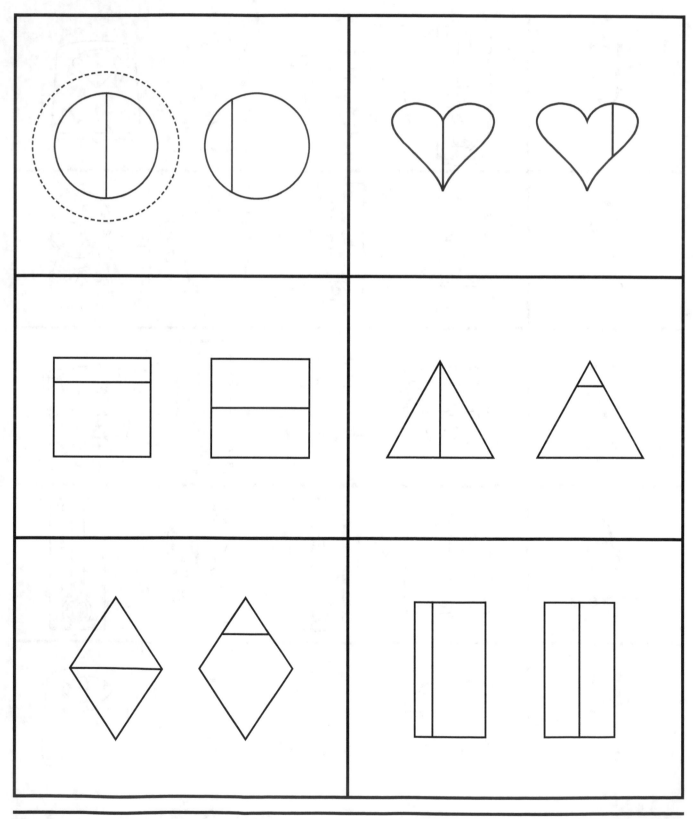

Equal Parts

Directions: Circle the shape that has equal parts.

Equal Parts

Directions: Color half of the pictures in each square red.

Name_____ Date_____

Fractions: 1/2

Directions: Color 1/2 of each shape.

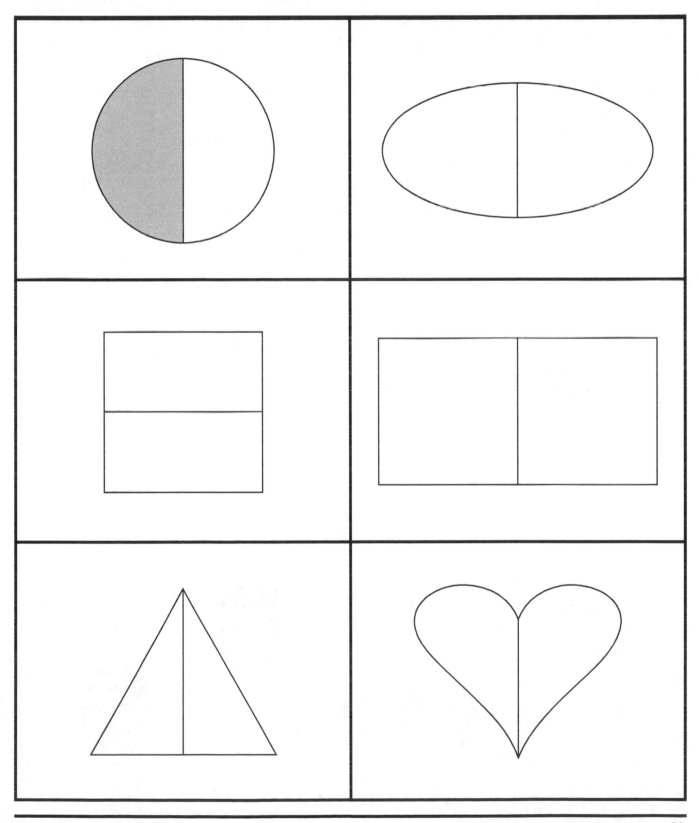

Name_____ Date_____

Fractions: 1/2

Directions: Color 1/2 of the pictures in each square with your favorite color.

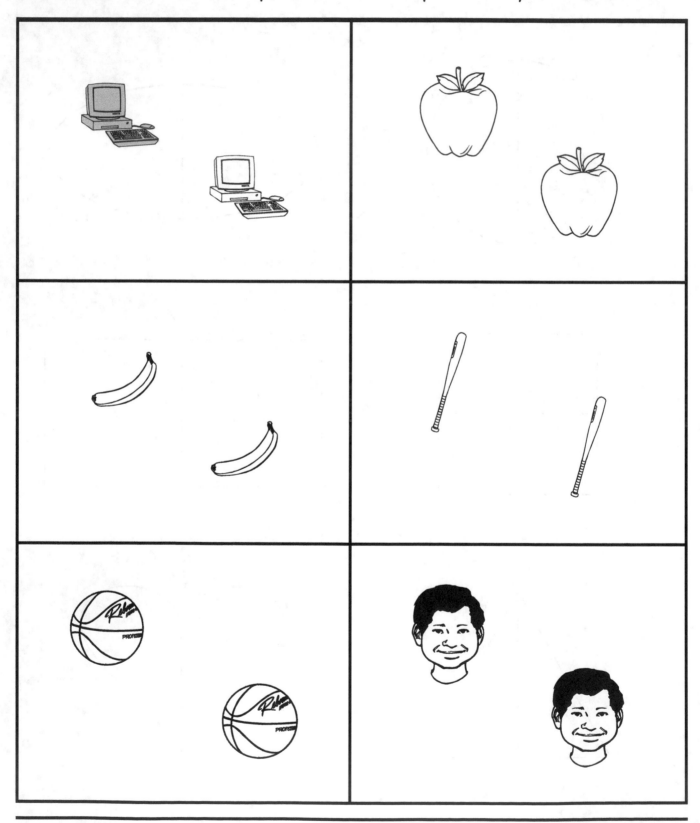

Name_____ Date_____

Fractions: 1/4

Directions: Color 1/4 of each shape.

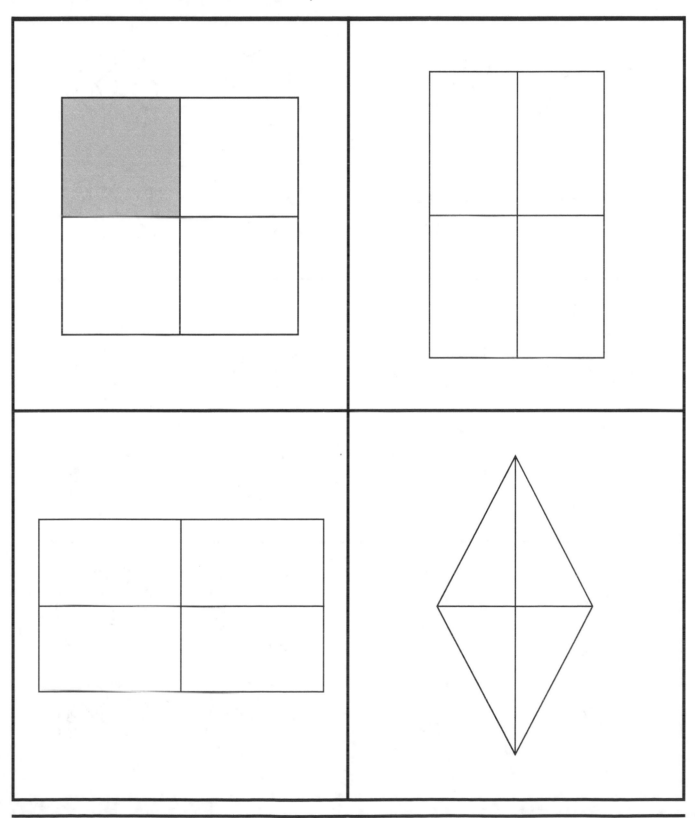

Name_____   Date_____

Fractions: 1/4

Directions: Color 1/4 of the pictures in each square with your favorite color.

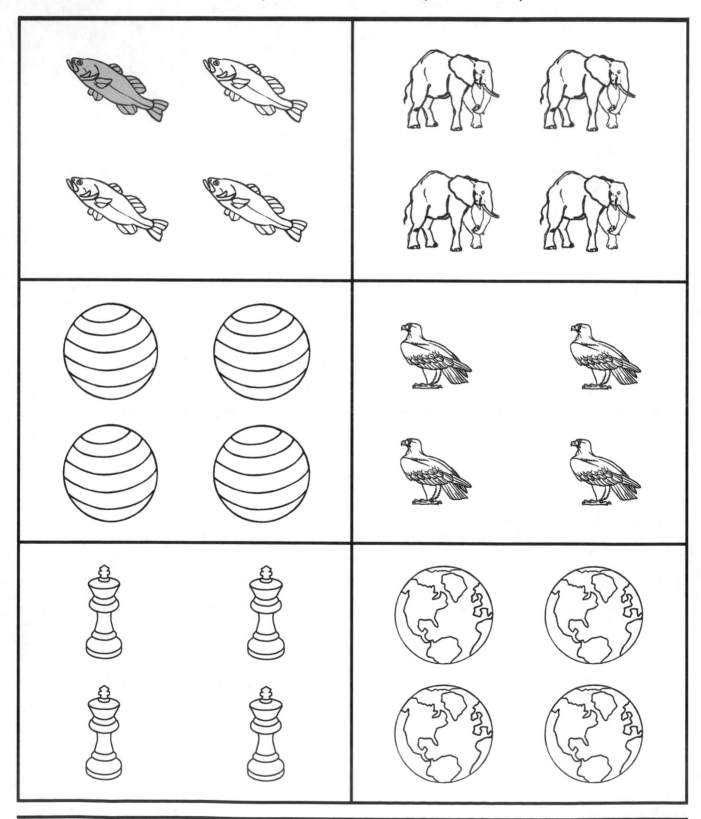

Fractions: 1/3

Directions: Color 1/3 of each shape.

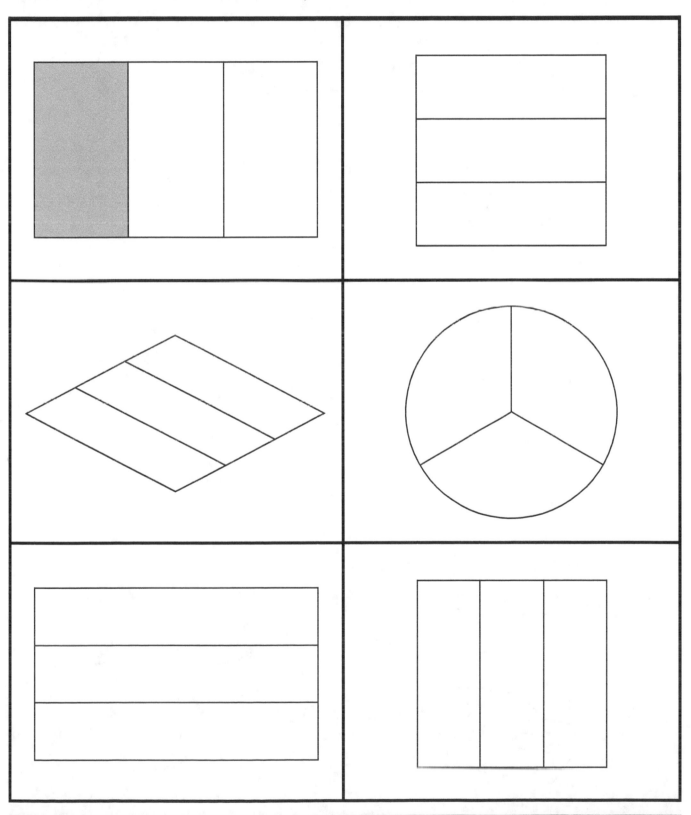

Name_____ Date_____

Fractions: 1/3

Directions: Color 1/3 of the pictures in each square with your favorite color.

Fractions

Directions: Circle the fraction that matches the picture.

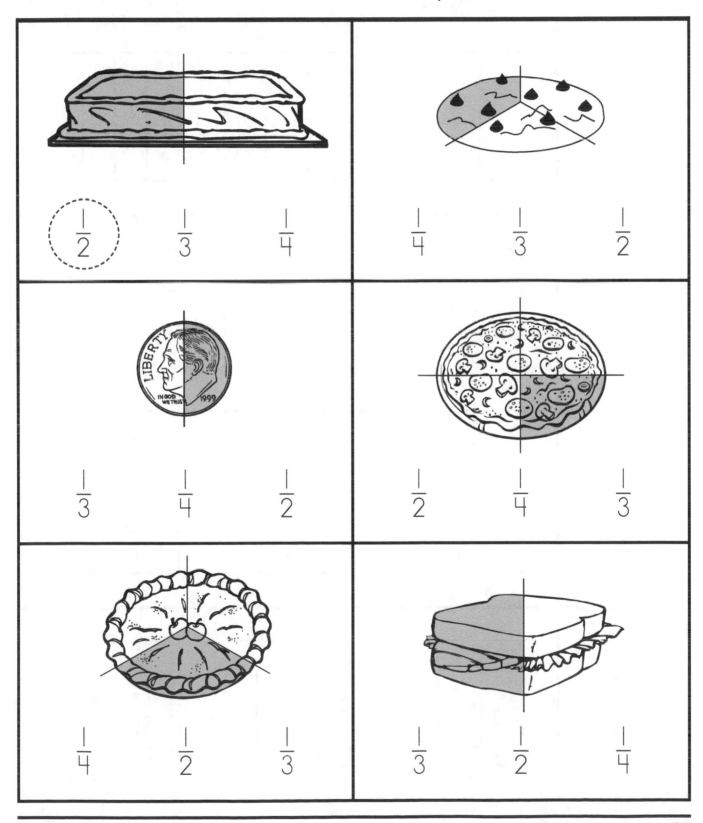

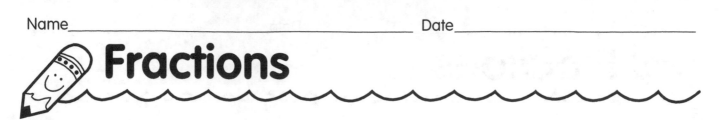

Fractions

Directions: Color the picture that matches the fraction.

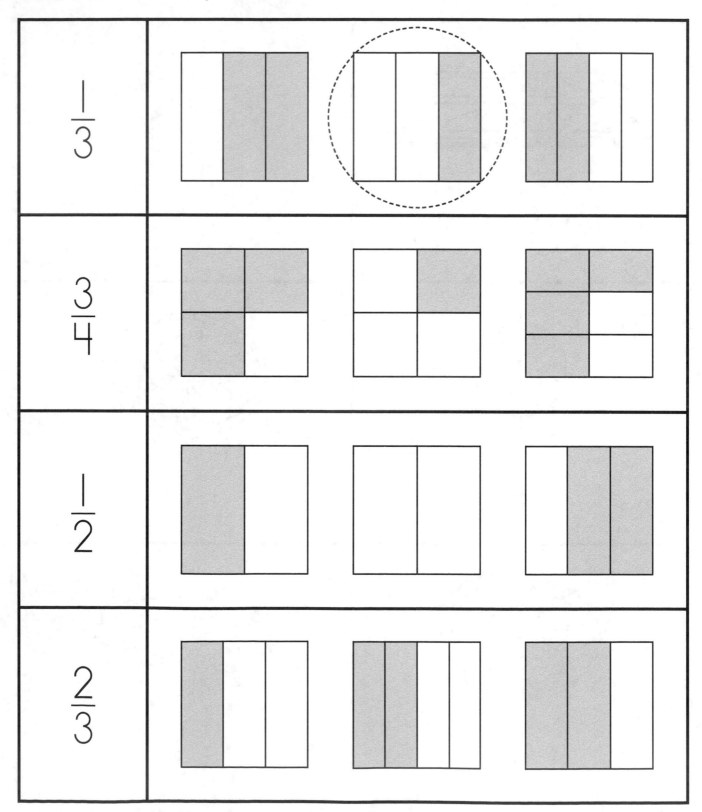

Fractions

Directions: Color the correct number of pictures to match the fraction.

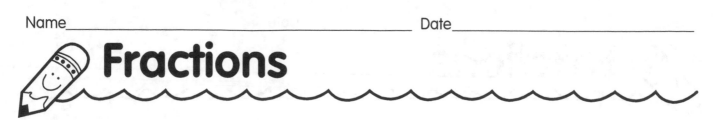

Fractions

Directions: Write the fraction that matches the number of shaded pictures.

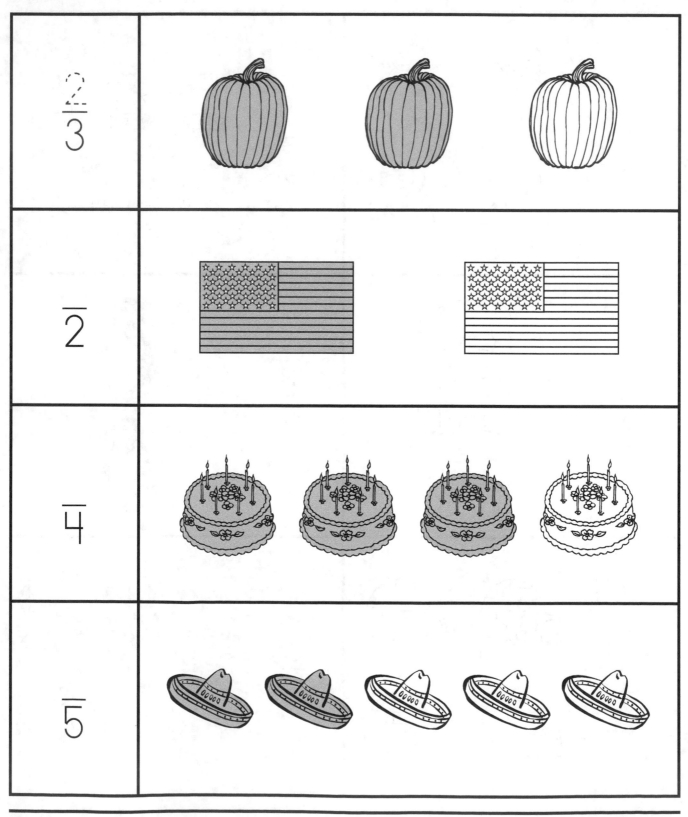

$\frac{2}{3}$

$\frac{}{2}$

$\frac{}{4}$

$\frac{}{5}$

Fractions

Directions: Write the fraction that matches the number of shaded parts.

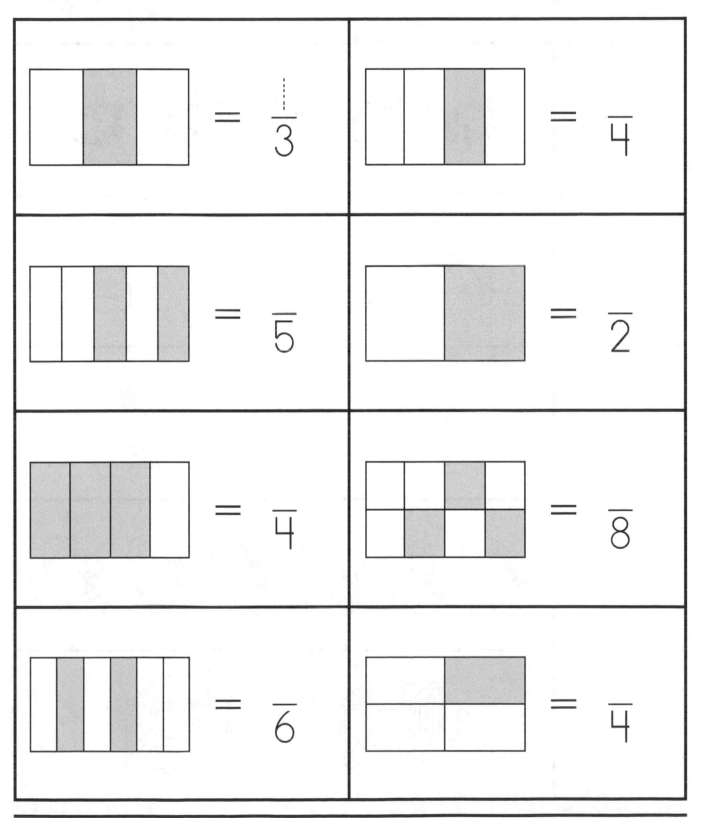

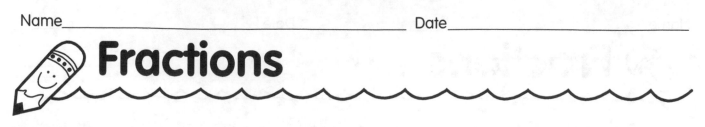

Fractions

Directions: Write your own fraction and shade the correct number of pictures.

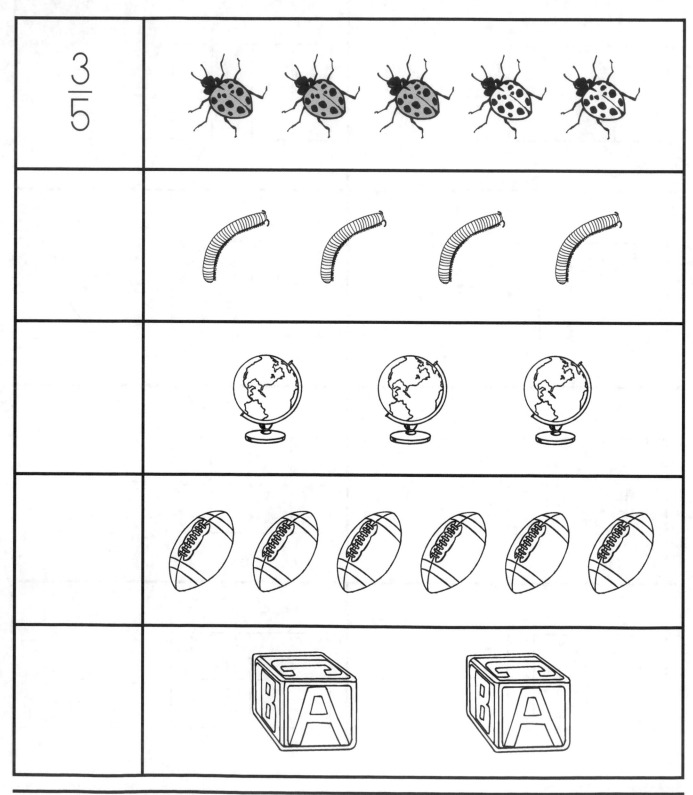

$\dfrac{3}{5}$

✏️ Graphing

Directions: Count the shapes and write the number.

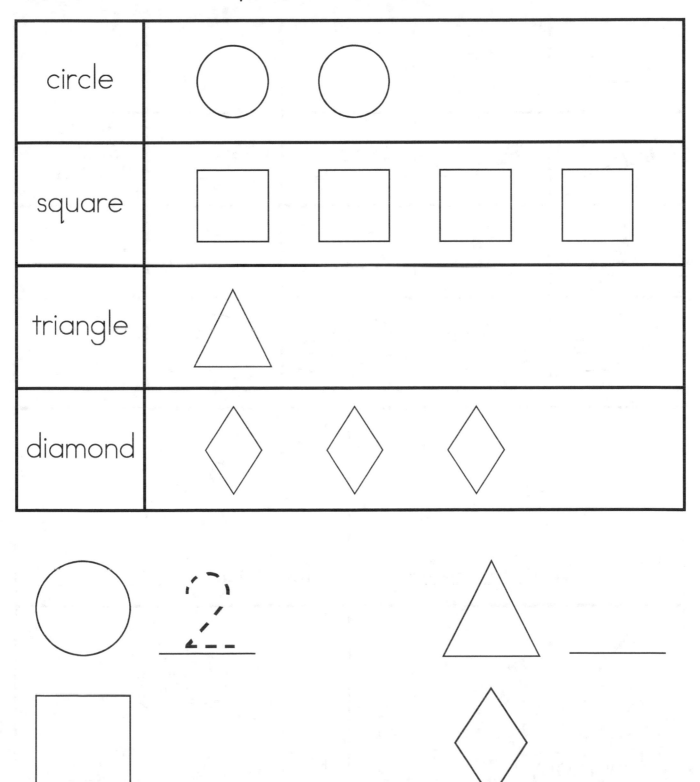

Graphing

Directions: Count the pictures and write the number.

How many? ___2___

How many? _____

How many? _____

How many? _____

Graphing

Directions: Count the pictures and write the number.

How many? ___3___

How many? _____

How many? _____

How many? _____

Graphing

Directions: Count the pictures and write the number.

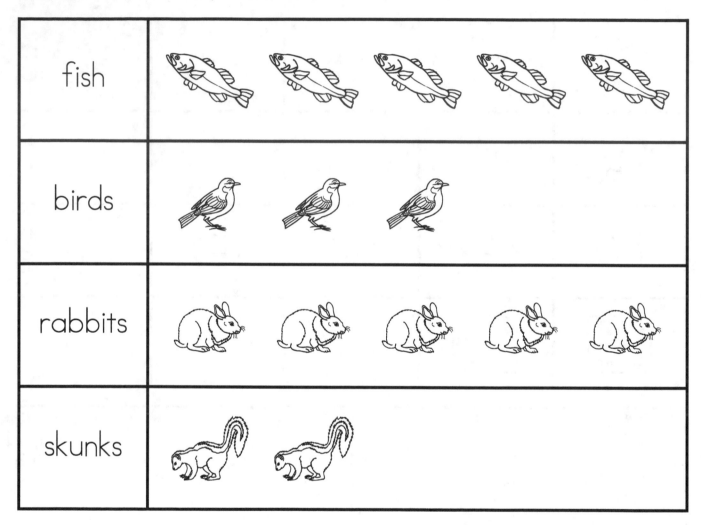

fish	
birds	
rabbits	
skunks	

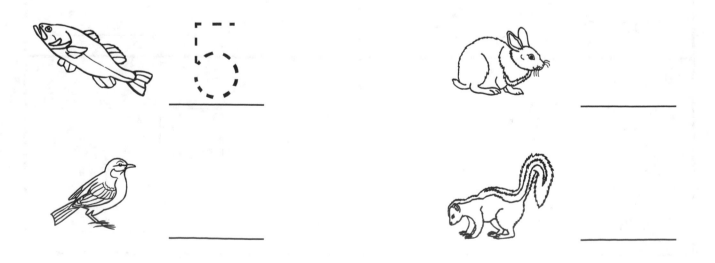

✏️ Graphing

Directions: Count the shirts. Then, count the shirts of each color and write the number.

brown	👕
red	👕 👕 👕
blue	👕 👕
green	👕 👕
yellow	👕 👕 👕 👕 👕

3 _____ red 👕   _____ blue 👕

_____ green 👕   _____ brown 👕

_____ yellow 👕

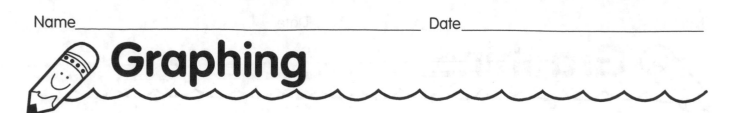

Graphing

Directions: Color the correct number of boxes for each picture.

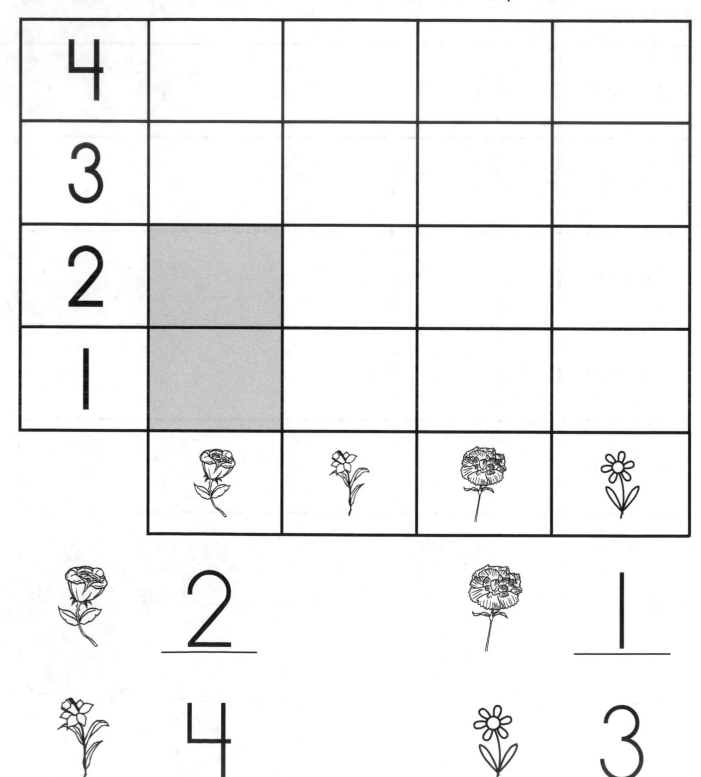

Name_____ Date_____

Graphing

Directions: Count the shaded boxes for each picture and write the number.

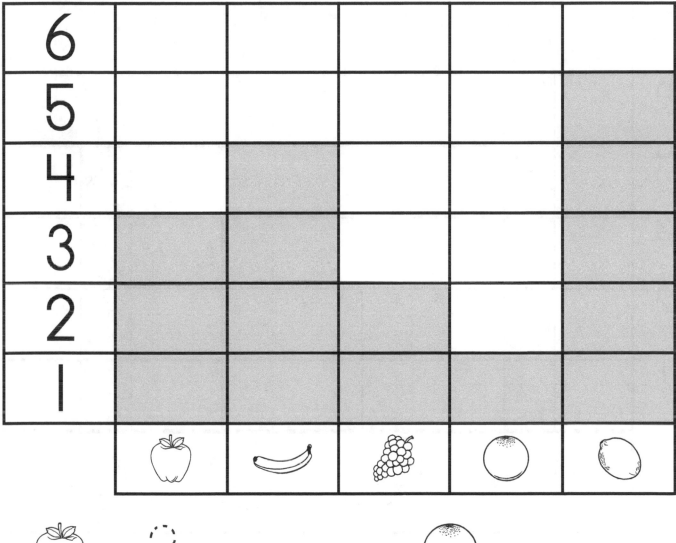

	🍎	🍌	🍇	🍊	🍋
6					
5					▓
4		▓			▓
3	▓	▓			▓
2	▓	▓	▓		▓
1	▓	▓	▓	▓	▓

🍎 _____

🍌 _____

🍇 _____

🍊 _____

🍋 _____

Graphing

Directions: Count the shaded boxes for each picture and write the number.

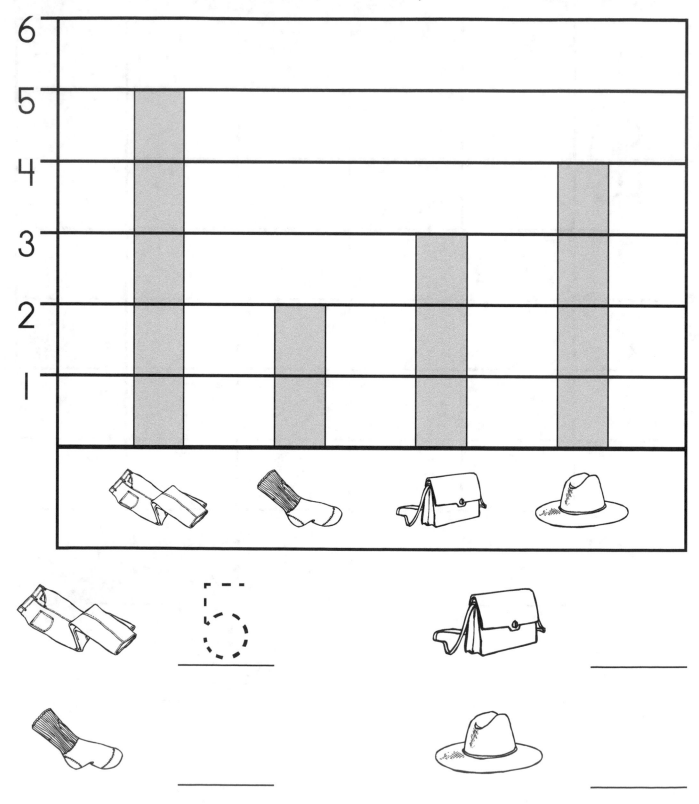

Graphing

Directions: Count the pizza slices and write the number of slices each person ate.

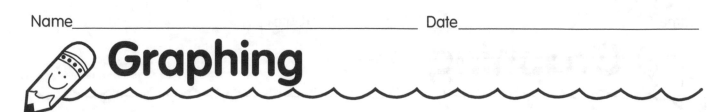

Graphing

Directions: Count the shaded boxes for each picture and write the number.

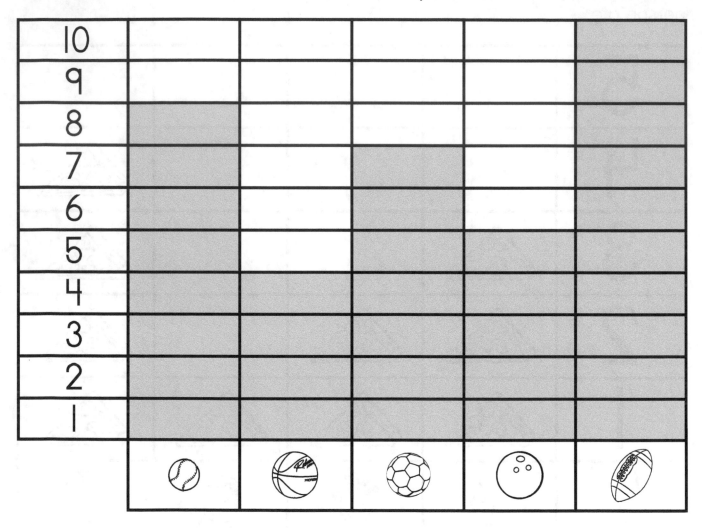

10					
9					
8					
7					
6					
5					
4					
3					
2					
1					

 _____

 _____

 _____

 _____

 _____

Name_____   Date_____

Graphing

Directions: Count the shaded boxes for each picture and write the number.

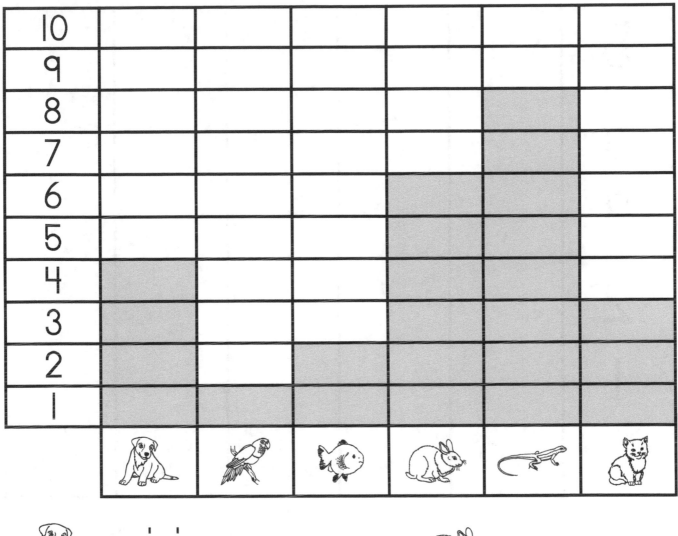

10						
9						
8					▓	
7					▓	
6				▓	▓	
5				▓	▓	
4	▓			▓	▓	
3	▓			▓	▓	▓
2	▓		▓	▓	▓	▓
1	▓	▓	▓	▓	▓	▓

  __4__

  _____

 _____

  _____

  _____

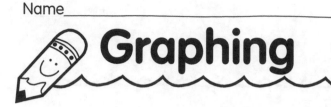

Graphing

Directions: Color the correct number of boxes for each picture.

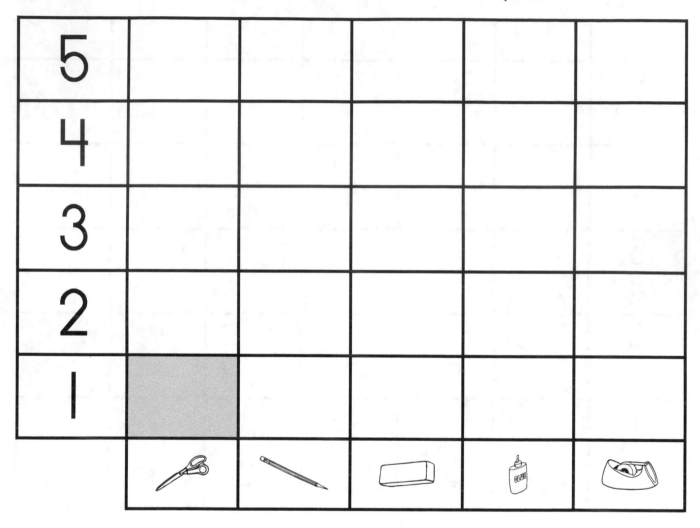

5					
4					
3					
2					
1					

 1

 5

[eraser] 4

 2

 3

Name_____ Date_____

Graphing

Directions: Color the correct number of boxes for each picture.

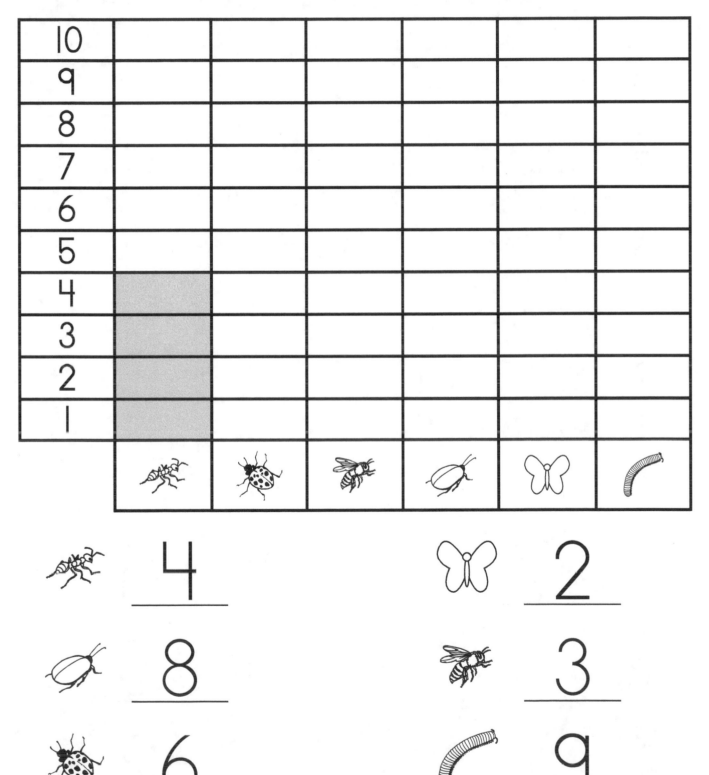

Name_____ Date_____

 # Graphing

Directions: Color the correct number of boxes for each picture.

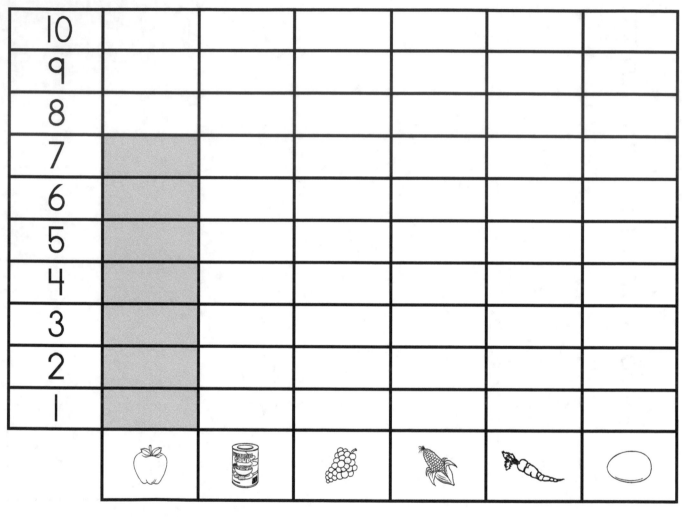

10						
9						
8						
7						
6						
5						
4						
3						
2						
1						

 7

 3

5

1

2

9

Graphing

Directions: Use the graph to draw the correct number of pictures in the box.

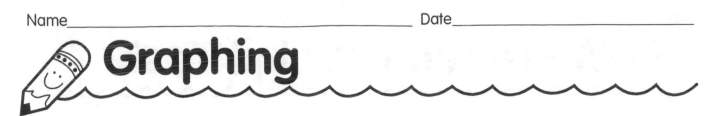

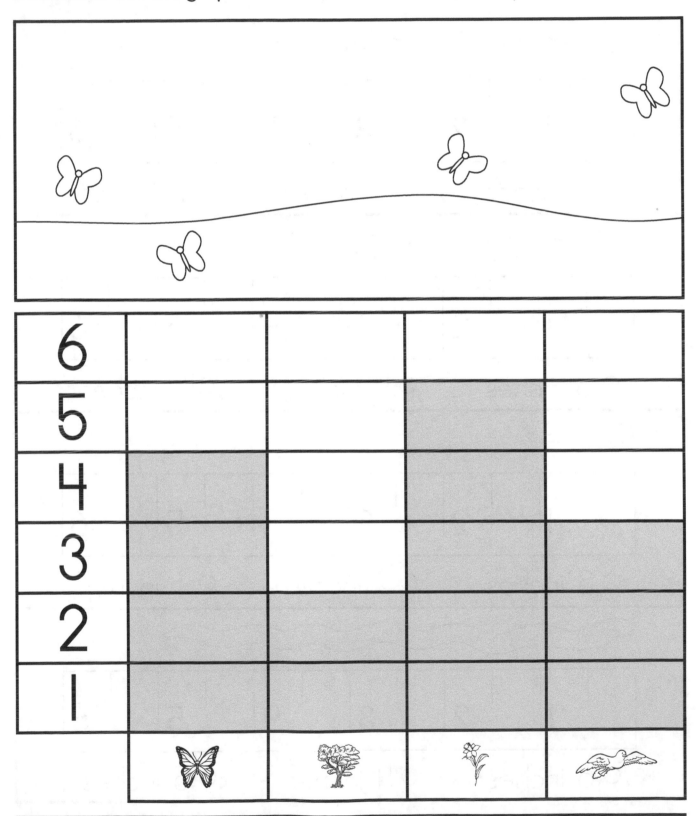

Measurement Unit Test

Directions: Fill in the circle next to the number of inches each worm measures.

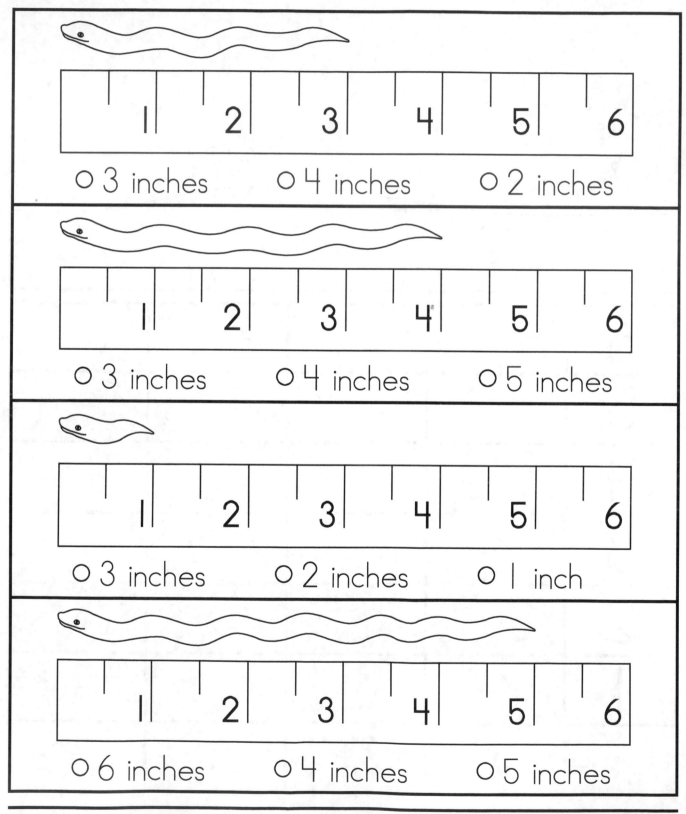

○ 3 inches   ○ 4 inches   ○ 2 inches

○ 3 inches   ○ 4 inches   ○ 5 inches

○ 3 inches   ○ 2 inches   ○ 1 inch

○ 6 inches   ○ 4 inches   ○ 5 inches

Measurement Unit Test

Directions: Fill in the circle next to the number of degrees each thermometer shows.

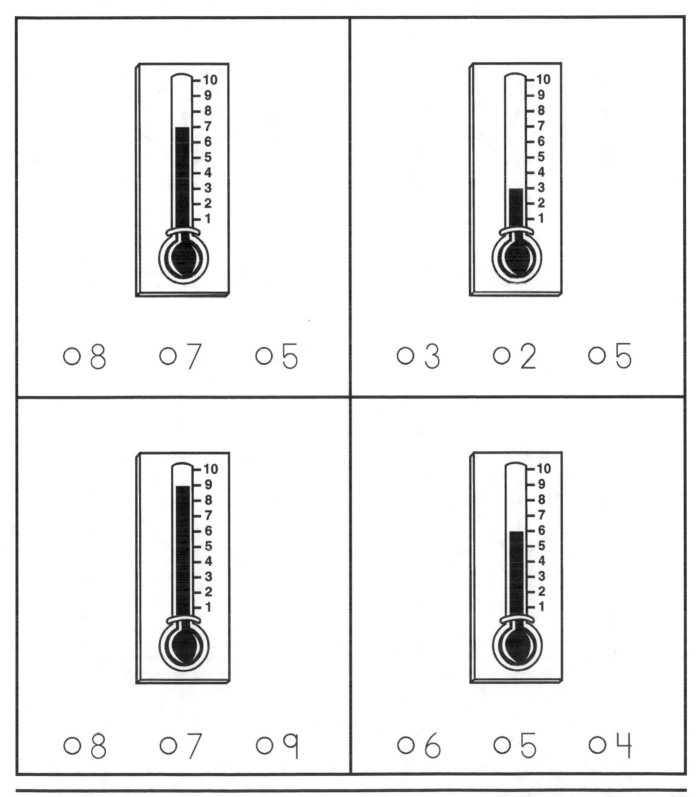

○ 8   ○ 7   ○ 5   ○ 3   ○ 2   ○ 5

○ 8   ○ 7   ○ 9   ○ 6   ○ 5   ○ 4

Measurement Unit Test

Directions: Fill in the circle next to the number of pounds each scale shows.

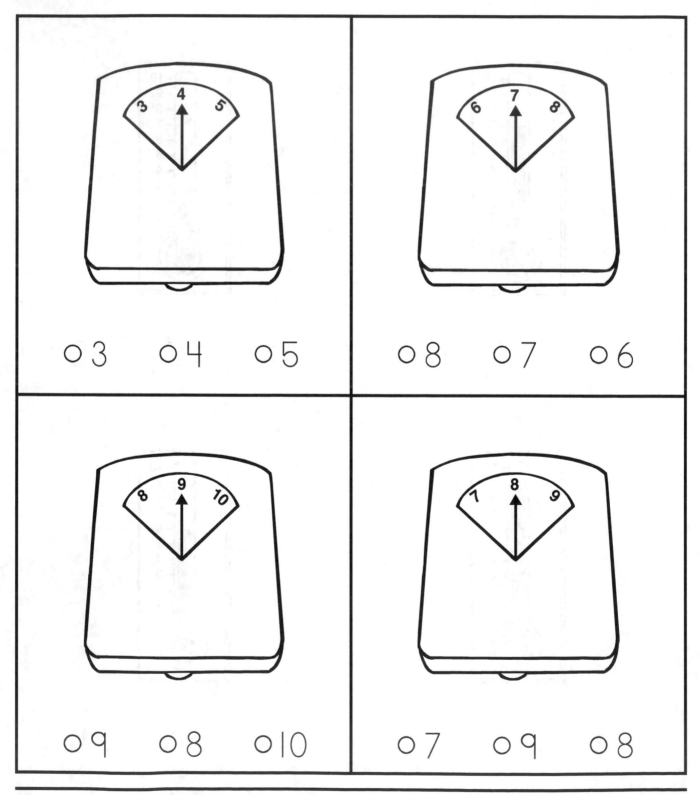

○ 3   ○ 4   ○ 5

○ 8   ○ 7   ○ 6

○ 9   ○ 8   ○ 10

○ 7   ○ 9   ○ 8

Fractions Unit Test

Directions: Fill in the circle next to the fraction that matches the picture.

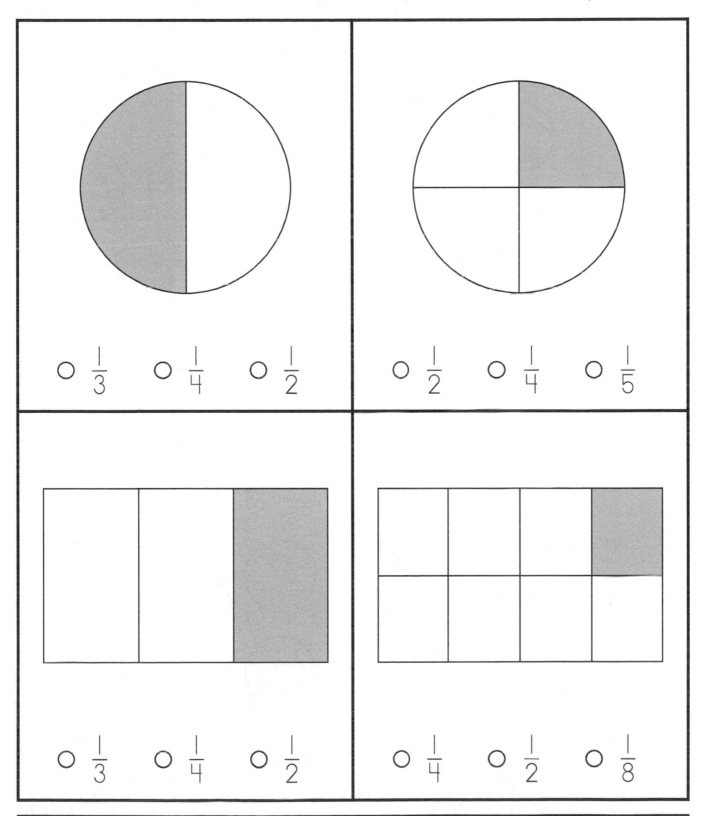

○ $\frac{1}{3}$ ○ $\frac{1}{4}$ ○ $\frac{1}{2}$ ○ $\frac{1}{2}$ ○ $\frac{1}{4}$ ○ $\frac{1}{5}$

○ $\frac{1}{3}$ ○ $\frac{1}{4}$ ○ $\frac{1}{2}$ ○ $\frac{1}{4}$ ○ $\frac{1}{2}$ ○ $\frac{1}{8}$

Name_____   Date_____

Fractions Unit Test

Directions: Fill in the circle next to the fraction that matches the pictures.

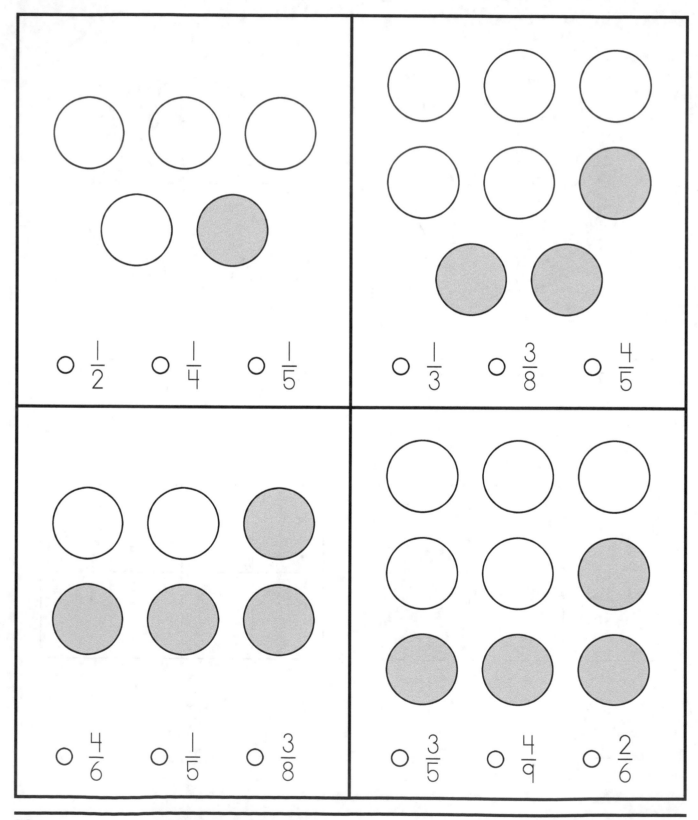

Fractions Unit Test

Directions: Fill in the circle next to the picture that matches the fraction.

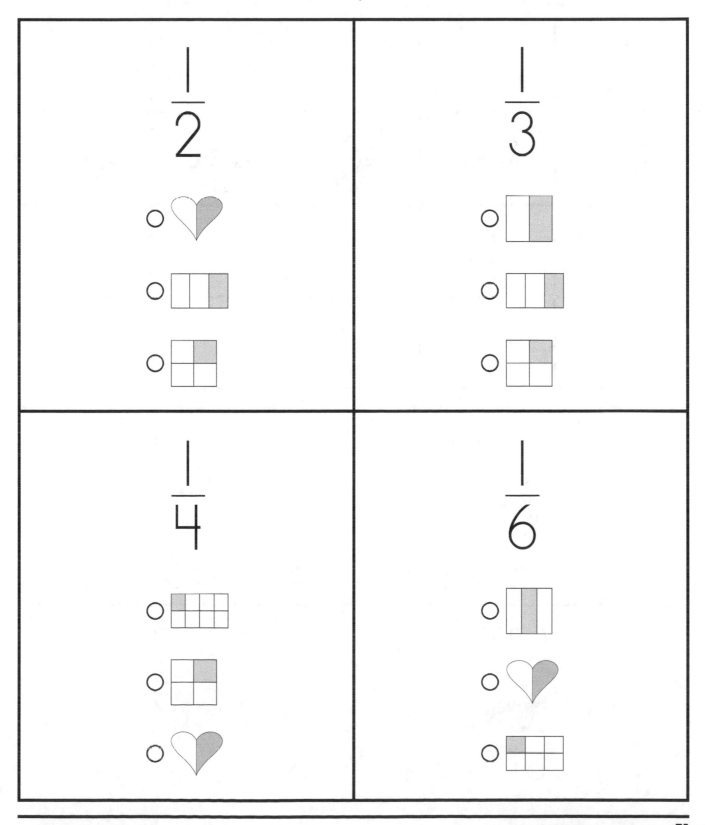

Name_____ Date_____

 Graphing Unit Test

Directions: Fill in the circle next to the number of pictures shown.

How many?

○ 4   ○ 2   ○ 3

How many?

○ 2   ○ 3   ○ 1

How many?

○ 5   ○ 4   ○ 3

How many?

○ 4   ○ 3   ○ 1

Graphing Unit Test

Directions: Fill in the circle next to the number of shaded boxes shown for each picture.

How many?

○ 3   ○ 1   ○ 2

How many?

○ 2   ○ 1   ○ 3

How many?

○ 4   ○ 5   ○ 3

How many?

○ 3   ○ 2   ○ 1

Graphing Unit Test

Directions: Fill in the circle next to the number of shaded boxes shown for each picture.

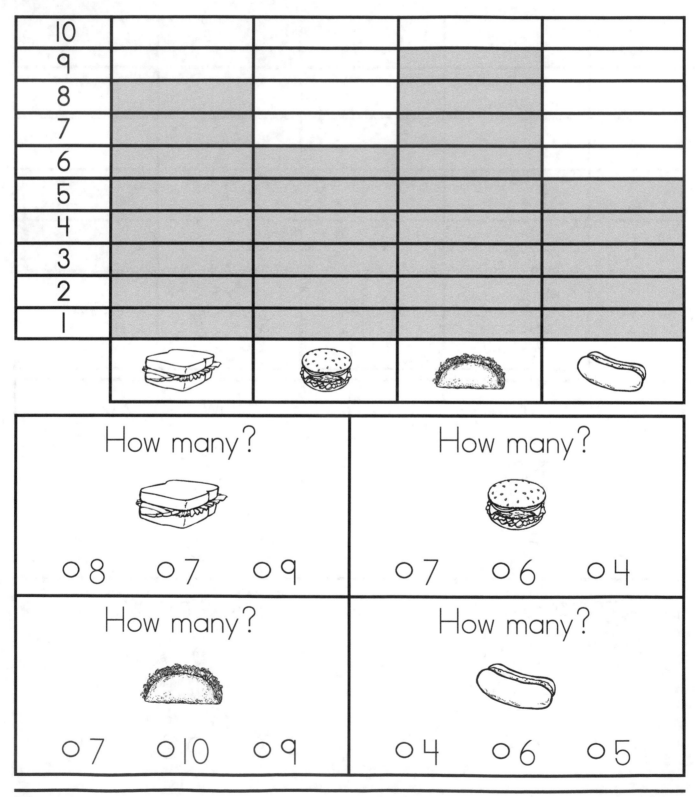

Measurement (page 1)
Directions: Write how many inches long each worm is.

- 3"
- 2"
- 6"
- 5"
- 4"

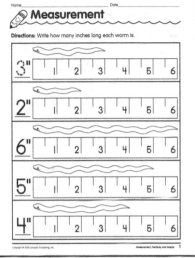

Measurement (page 2)
Directions: Use a ruler to measure. Write how many inches long each picture is.

- 4"
- 3"
- 1"
- 5"
- 2"

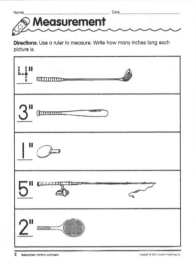

Measurement (page 3)
Directions: Write the number of degrees each thermometer shows.

2 degrees	4 degrees
6 degrees	1 degree
5 degrees	3 degrees
10 degrees	7 degrees
8 degrees	9 degrees

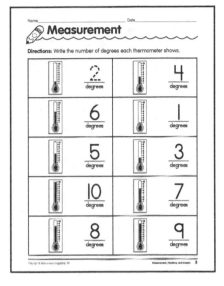

Measurement (page 4)
Directions: Color each thermometer to match the number of degrees.

- 5 degrees
- 3 degrees
- 6 degrees
- 8 degrees
- 2 degrees

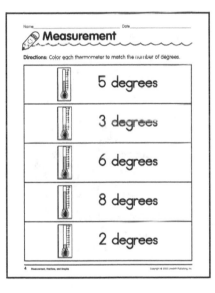

Measurement (page 5)
Directions: Circle the thermometer that matches the number of degrees.

- 2 degrees
- 5 degrees
- 3 degrees
- 8 degrees
- 6 degrees

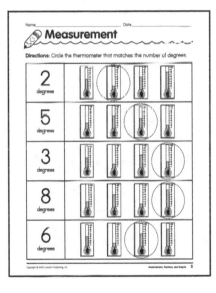

Measurement (page 6)
Directions: Write the number of cups that are in each measuring cup.

- 1 cup
- 2 cups
- 5 cups
- 3 cups
- 4 cups

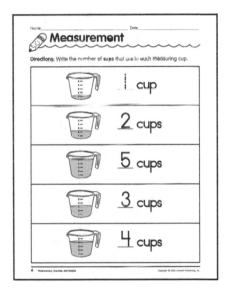

Measurement (page 7)
Directions: Color each measuring cup to match the number of cups.

- 3 cups
- 4 cups
- 2 cups
- 5 cups
- 1 cup

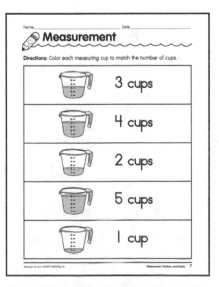

Measurement (page 8)
Directions: Circle the measuring cup that matches the number of cups.

- 5 cups
- 1 cup
- 4 cups
- 3 cups
- 2 cups

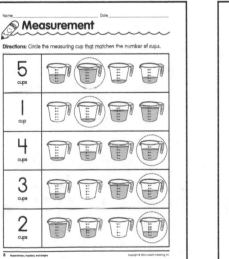

Measurement (page 9)
Directions: Write the number of pounds that are shown on each scale.

- 6 pounds
- 4 pounds
- 9 pounds
- 2 pounds
- 5 pounds

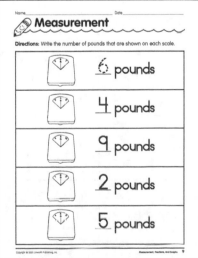

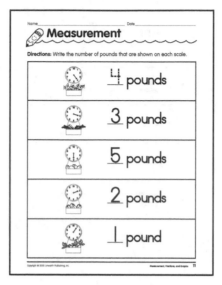

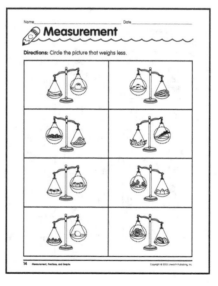

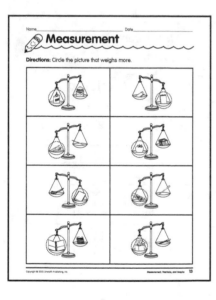

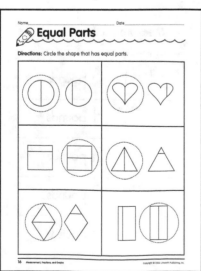

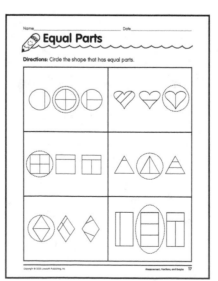

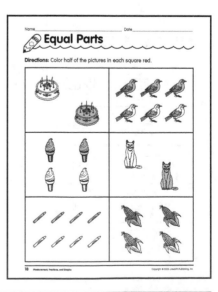

Answer Key pages 19–27

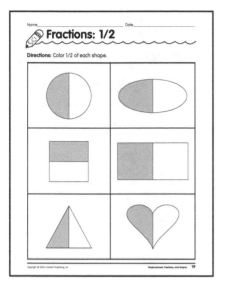

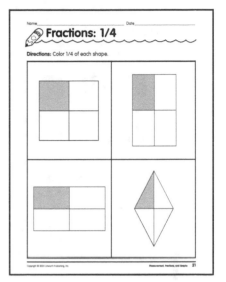

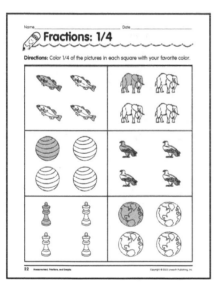

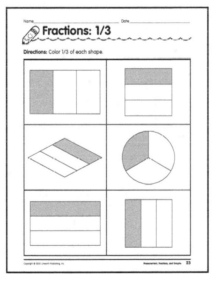

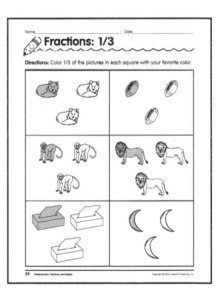

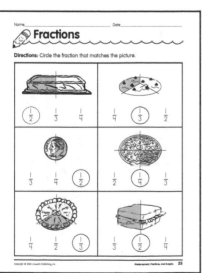

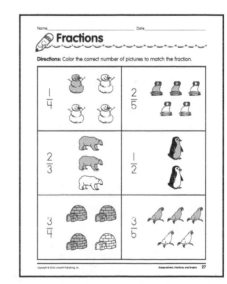

Answer Key pages 28–36

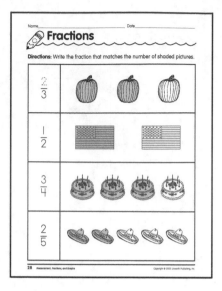

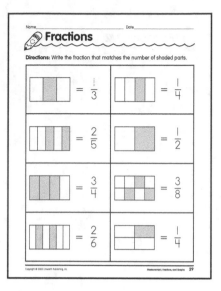

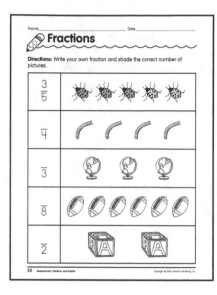

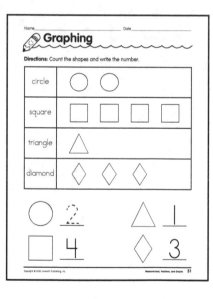

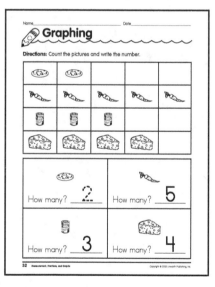

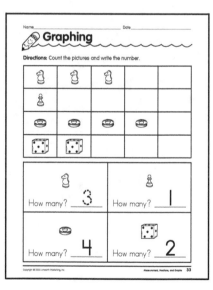

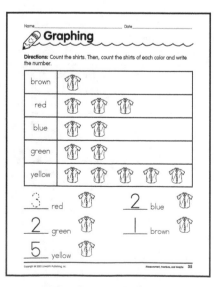

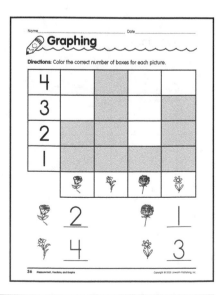

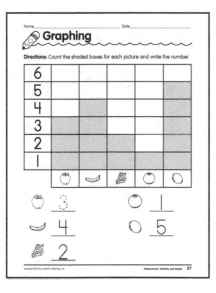

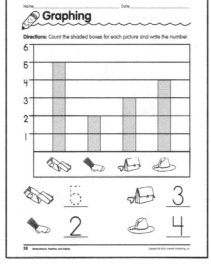

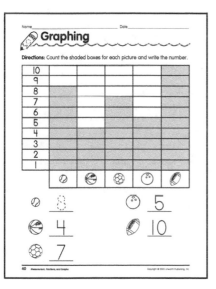

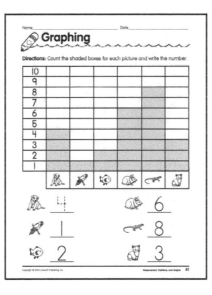

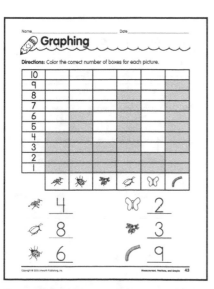

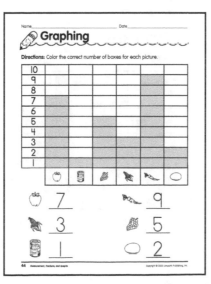

Answer Key pages 46–54

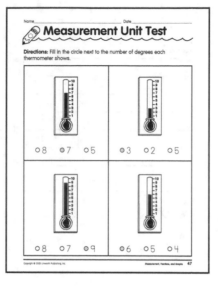
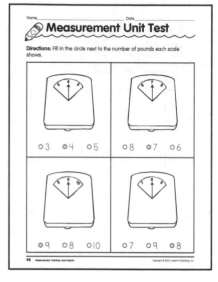
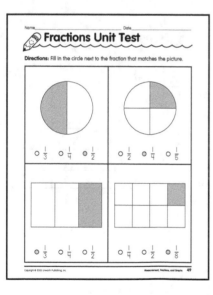
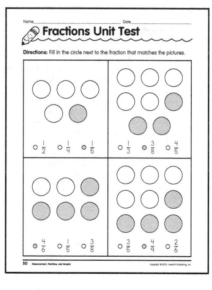
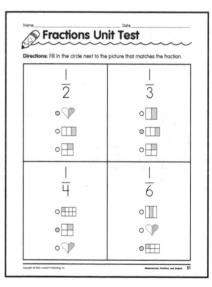
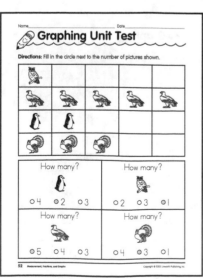
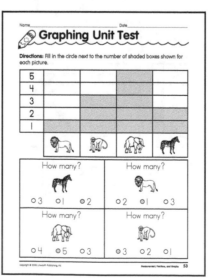
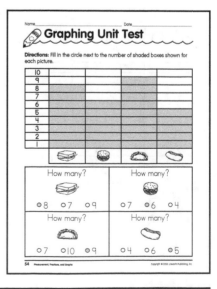

9 781586 831424